The Basics Of Agile and Lean

ADITI AGARWAL

The Basics Of Agile and Lean   Aditi Agarwal

Text copyright © 2019 Aditi Agarwal

All rights reserved.

No part of this book may be reproduced or transmitted in any form or by any means, electronic, mechanical, magnetic, or photographic, including photocopying, recording, or by any information storage or retrieval system or otherwise, without express written permission of the publisher. No warranty liability whatsoever is assumed for the use of the information contained herein. Although every precaution has been taken in the preparation of this book, the publisher and author assume no responsibility for errors or omissions.

Published By: Aditi Agarwal Books LLC
Date of Publication: Feb 2019
Last Revision: Jan 2021
Language: English

FREE *Membership to the Agile and Lean Leaders Mentoring Network (ALLMN)*

Be a mentor, or learn from experienced Agile and Lean leaders by subscribing to the exclusive Agile and Lean Leaders Facebook Network for Free:

www.facebook.com/groups/AgileLeanLeaders/

To God for his blessings
To my family for their loving support

Table of Contents

Introduction 6
Acknowledgments 10
Chapter 1 – What is Agile? 11
Chapter 2 – The Agile Manifesto 26
Chapter 3 – The Agile Principles 31
Chapter 4 – Agile Frameworks 42
Chapter 5 – Scaling Agile 55
Chapter 6 – What is Lean? 78
Chapter 7 – House of Lean 93
Chapter 8 – Agile or Lean 102
Bibliography 109
Recommended Reading 110
About Me 112
More Books by the Author 113
Post Your Review 117

Introduction

People often debate whether Agile and Lean are the same or different. Sometimes, people ask which one is the best methodology for their organization. This book is written to introduce you to the core values and principles of both Agile and Lean and will hopefully answer your questions on these methodologies.

Who Should Read This Book?

Anyone interested in being Agile should read this book. Anyone who wants to adopt lean thinking would benefit from this book. Here are a few roles that would derive the most value from this product.

- Agile coaches
- Agile or Lean leaders
- Lean managers
- Lean-Agile manager-thinkers
- Scrum masters (SMs)
- Product owners (POs)
- Release train engineers (RTEs)
- SAFe Agilists (SAs)
- SAFe program consultants (SPCs)
- Product managers
- Project managers

- System architects
- UX designers
- Test managers or engineers
- System analysts
- Lean or Agile team members
- Students seeking a corporate job

Why Did I Write This Book?

Being an Agile Coach and an experienced Scrum Master for a software development organization, I provide recommendations to teams to adopt an agile mindset and to embrace lean thinking. However, I discovered many people are ignorant of Lean and are often confused with the similarities and differences between Agile and Lean methodologies.

Another reason for writing this book is that most teams follow Agile practices but fail to deliver the business value. The reason being that these teams are doing Agile vs being Agile. This book will re-emphasize the importance of the core values in the Agile Manifesto and Agile principles. Embracing these principles in day-to-day work will increase the team's agility. Similarly, Lean teams must embrace the core principles of Lean methodology and adopt Lean thinking in making business decisions.

This book is an attempt to answer some of the popular questions such as:

- What is Agile?
- What is Lean?
- Which is better? Agile or Lean?
- What are the 12 Agile Principles?
- What is the Agile Manifesto?
- What is Scrum?
- What is the difference between Agile and Scrum?
- What is Kanban?
- Is Kanban Lean or Agile?
- What is the Toyota Production System?
- What are the different versions of the Toyota House of Lean?
- How many Agile frameworks are there?
- How are Lean and Agile different?
- How is Lean and Agile the same?

I wrote this simple and concise reference book so that you can take it anywhere you like and read it whenever you want.

I hope this book will serve as a good starting point on your journey to master Agile and Lean. This book will also help you decide when and when not to adopt Agile or Lean.

How to Use This Book?

If you are new to Agile or Lean, I recommend that you read this book from front to back. For those who are more familiar with these methodologies, you can use this book as a reference guide or a handbook.

If you are more interested in being agile, I recommend that you read Chapter 3 – The Agile Principles. If you are interested to compare Lean with Agile, jump to Chapter 8 – Agile or Lean.

Let's get started

Set aside a few hours each day to be Agile or to develop Lean thinking, or both. The chapters that follow describe the two most popular methodologies to deliver work effectively.

Hope that you have as much fun reading as I had in writing this book. Happy Reading!

Acknowledgments

First, I would like to express my gratitude to God whose blessings inspired me to write this book. I strongly believe in sharing my knowledge and helping others to succeed.

I would like to acknowledge the support of my parents who have always believed in me. Their unconditional love gave me the courage to complete this work.

This book would not have been possible without the support of my husband. I will take this opportunity to thank him for his continued support and encouragement.

Then, a special thanks to my son whose curious questions inspired me to share my knowledge and teach a complex subject in a simple manner.

I also thank my colleagues, my friends, and my mentors who trust my abilities and knowledge to write this book.

Chapter 1 – What is Agile?

"We cannot make informed decisions or create a quality product without first understanding why we are doing what we are doing."
  - *Jim Benson*

This chapter sets the foundation to understand the Agile methodology and to be agile. It also answers some of your frequently asked questions on Agile and its benefits.

What Is Agile?

Agile is a set of management practices that enable organizations to build software iteratively and incrementally with an emphasis on collaboration, responding to change, and continuous improvement. Its core foundation was laid with the **Agile Manifesto for Software Development** in 2001.

Agile is now spreading to all types of organizations and every aspect of work as quoted in a Harvard Business Review article, **Embracing Agile**, written by Darrell K. Rigby, Jeff Sutherland, and Hirakata Takeuchi in 2016. The HBR article states, "*In today's world of increased complexity, volatility, turbulence, and ambiguity, the Agile methodology uncovers better ways to develop complex products and master continuous change.*"

The Agile methodology is a set of methods and practices based on the **Agile Manifesto** and the **12 Agile Principles**. Chapter 4 introduces the different Agile frameworks.

Origins of Agile

From 1970 to 1990, problems became evident with the "waterfall" methodology and software thought leaders became frustrated. During this period, new foundational theories and software development practices started to emerge.

In 1984, Barry W. Boehm published an article, "*Prototyping vs. Specifying - A multi-project experiment*", with experimental data showing better results with prototyping for software product development.

Another article, "_Knowledge-based communication processes in software engineering_", written by Gerhard Fisher and Matthias Schneider stressed the importance of communication and incremental design.

In 1985, Tob Gilb published an article to expose the theoretical and practical aspects of the first alternative approach to the "waterfall" method, the _Evolutionary Delivery Model, or Evo._

In 1986, Takeuchi and Nonaka publish their article "_The New New Product Development Game_" in Harvard Business Review. They stressed the importance of teams and highlighted some analogies between a team sport like rugby and the new game of product development. In rugby football, a Scrum refers to a tightly packed formation of players with their heads down who attempt to gain possession of the ball. This article set the foundation for the Scrum framework.

In 1991, James Martin described the timebox approach in his book, _Rapid Application Development._

In 1993, Jeff Sutherland invents the incremental and iterative development approach, _Scrum_, as an alternative to the "waterfall" methodology at Easel Corporation.

In 1994, software development experts met in London and formed a DSDM consortium to jointly develop and promote an independent RAD framework.

In 1995, Ken Schwaber and Jeff Sutherland co-presented Scrum at the OOPSLA conference.

In 1996, the first Extreme Programming project was started under the leadership of Kent Beck. Later in 1999, Kent published an IEEE article, _Embracing Change with Extreme Programming_, describing rules of simple design. He also wrote a book, "_Extreme Programming Explained_" to present his experiences with Extreme Programming (XP).

In 2000, Martin Fowler published an extensive article on the importance and benefits of "_Continuous Integration_".

On Feb 11-13, 2001, 17 visionaries met at The Lodge at Snowbird ski resort in the Wasatch mountains of Utah to find common ground among different approaches to software development. These were representatives from

Extreme Programming, Scrum, DSDM, Adaptive Software Development, Crystal, and Feature-Driven Development. The outcome was a *Manifesto for Agile Software Development* that was signed by all participants.

Agile or agile?

What's the difference between **Agile** and **agile**? One with an uppercase 'A' and the other with a lowercase 'a'. This is quite confusing to many people. Let's compare the two and summarize the differences here.

The uppercase '**Agile**' denotes different frameworks such as Scrum, Extreme Programming, Crystal, etc. whereas the lowercase '**agile**' represents the core values such as collaboration, continuous improvement, experimentation, value delivery, and so on. The lowercase '**agile**' is about the results regardless of the technique.

The uppercase '**Agile**' is all about '**go/do Agile**' whereas the lowercase '**agile**' is more about '**being agile**' or '**being able to move or change quickly and easily**'.

It is easier to deploy '**Agile**' methods with adequate training and resources; however, it takes a considerable amount of time to be **'agile'** or to grow the organization **'agility'**.

Benefits of Agile

Agile methods help teams perform work effectively and efficiently while delivering a high-quality and valuable product. Some of the core benefits are listed as follows:

- Faster time to market
- Reduced mismatch
- High-performing and motivated teams
- Better collaboration
- Delighted customers
- Frequent feedback
- Continuous improvement
- Innovation and experimentation
- Embracing change
- High productivity
- Better quality
- Transparency
- Value delivery
- Sustainable pace

Faster time to market
Many large enterprises have transitioned to the Agile methodology and have reported

significant improvements in productivity and time-to-market. Agile methods are inherently designed to foster innovation, continuous improvement, better quality, shorter customer feedback loop, and faster time-to-market.
All Agile practices encourage splitting work into smaller, manageable pieces, prioritizing work to deliver the **maximum business value,** and developing the product **iteratively** and **incrementally**. This results in increasing the time-to-market by 30-75%.

Reduced mismatch
With the traditional plan-driven "waterfall" method, there is often a lot of mismatch between the approved requirements and the final delivered product. Often, end-users of the product are unhappy with the final product. On the other hand, developers become dis-interested and de-motivated due to dissatisfied customers despite their hard work throughout the development process.

Agile frameworks are based on shorter development cycles or **iterations** that allow sponsors, business owners, and other stakeholders to review the incremental work completed by the development team at the end of each iteration. This frequent review or the inspection process helps to minimize differences between business needs and the product.

High-performing and motivated teams
Agile methods create the conditions for high-performing and self-motivated teams to flourish. Being able to make decisions, work in an open, transparent environment, continuously learn, innovate, develop mastery of their skills, connect with the bigger picture, understand business goals, and collaborate are some of the conditions that contribute directly to being a high-performing, happy, and a self-motivated team.

A high-performing team is accountable and committed to common goals that are organized and prioritized via a product backlog.

Better collaboration
One of the core values of Agile is to focus on people interactions and face-to-face conversations. This emphasis on individuals and interactions allows clear, efficient, and effective communications, making Agile a people-centric framework.

Delighted customers
Agile methods promote early and continuous delivery of a valuable product that leads to delighted customers. The Agile practices of

regular inspection, frequent feedback, prioritization, and responding to change result in customer satisfaction and delight.

Frequent feedback
With the traditional plan-driven "waterfall" approach, customers are not able to provide their feedback on the product until the test phase. Late customer feedback results in late learning and expensive rework.

With Agile, customers get the opportunity to provide feedback at the end of every iteration. This allows the team to quickly adapt to the feedback.

Continuous improvement
Agile methods promote a continuous improvement culture. Systematic **inspect and adapt** practices encourage continuous improvement, thereby, fostering an environment of learning and growth.

Innovation and experimentation
In this fast-paced environment with ever-changing technology solutions, companies that adopt Agile frameworks are more likely to meet customer needs, develop innovative products, and sustain a competitive advantage.

Instead of choosing a single solution upfront, Agile methods encourage exploration of **multiple design options** and elimination of inadequate choices over time.

Embracing change
One of the core values of Agile is to respond to change and embrace it. Agile methods encourage re-prioritization of the product backlog at any time. Early feedback, continuous improvement, and the ability to embrace change is built-in to all Agile methods.

High productivity
The Agile approach boosts productivity through efficient interactions and face-to-face communications between individuals. Working on only a few prioritized items each iteration helps the team to narrow down its focus and develop high-quality software.

Better quality
One of the 12 Agile principles is, "Continuous attention to technical excellence and good design enhances agility". Built-in quality is a core principle of Agile and requires ongoing training and commitment.

Agile practices such as continuous integration, continuous delivery, test first, pair programming, test-driven development, and defining a scalable definition of done help to achieve a high-quality architecture, design, and code. Built-in quality leads to better predictability, improved performance, reduced rework, and higher customer satisfaction.

Transparency
Transparency is built on trust between the business and development. Without mutual trust, other Agile benefits such as high-performing teams, innovation, continuous improvement, etc. will cease to exist. Agile frameworks build **trust and transparency** via practices such as establishing a common understanding of the product roadmap, objectives, and goals, providing visibility into the team's velocity, routinely meeting sprint commitments, inspect and adapt, and more.

Value delivery
One of the Agile principles is, "Our highest priority is to satisfy the customer through early and continuous delivery of a valuable software." Agile frameworks target maximizing the value for the product and delivering a valuable product to end-users.

There are many ways in which product value can be measured. It is important to align and measure the Key Value Indicators (KVI) for your product. Agile practices such as **release-**

on-demand encourage Product Owners or the business to measure Key Performance Indicators (KPIs) or Key Value Indicators (KVIs) early and often.

Sustainable pace
Agile methods encourage development at a pace that a team would be able to sustain indefinitely. With Agile, the development team decides how many user stories can be brought into the sprint backlog.

One of the Agile principles is dedicated to 'sustainable pace' and states, "Agile processes promote sustainable development. The sponsors, developers, and users should be able to maintain a **constant pace** indefinitely."

Common Agile Myths

There are many myths about Agile that are prevalent these days. Some of the common myths are listed as follows:

Myth #1: Agile is anti-documentation
While some people believe that Agile doesn't need any documentation, that's hardly the truth. Agile recommends creating **just-in-time** and valuable documentation rather than creating bulky upfront documentation. If

documentation adds value, it needs to be prioritized the same way as other user stories.

Myth #2: Agile involves no planning
Agile does not encourage detailed upfront planning, but it does recommend creating a product roadmap to visualize and align on product priorities. Apart from this, Agile teams also participate in iteration planning and release planning. Agile is not anti-planning, but it's **anti-static planning** or against establishing firm commitments.

Myth #3: Agile does not need design/architecture
Some people believe that Agile teams do not focus on architecture and design. This is a common myth. Agile frameworks encourage teams to build products with a simple design and to add design complexity only when needed. Agile does not support the huge upfront design but encourages an **emergent design** that continually evolves to meet current and future business needs.

Myth #4: Agile can solve any problem
Another common myth is that Agile frameworks can solve all problems. The fact is that it is possible to fail with Agile, but you **fail faster** with Agile as compared to the traditional plan-driven "waterfall" approach.

Though Agile methods encourage teams to develop on cadence, drive maximum business value, bring transparency, and create high-performing teams, these benefits cannot be sustained without an agile mindset.

Myth #5: Agile is only relevant for software development efforts

The Agile Manifesto was formulated especially for software development efforts in 2001. Thus, many people think that Agile is only effective for the software industry. However, Agile frameworks are being widely adopted within different types of organizations. Irrespective of the type of work, every organization needs to respond to changing market needs, encourage people interactions, build collaboratively, and drive continuous improvement.

Exercise 1: Test your knowledge

- What is Agile?
- What do you understand by being agile?

Exercise 2: Brainstorming

Brainstorm with your team and write down the top two Agile benefits that would drive your organization or portfolio to be agile.

Chapter 2 – The Agile Manifesto

"Success today requires the agility and drive to constantly rethink, reinvigorate, react, and reinvent."
- *Bill Gates*

In this chapter, let's discuss the core values contained in the **Agile Manifesto for software development**.

What Is "The Agile Manifesto"?

The Agile Manifesto states:

We are uncovering better ways of developing software by doing it and helping others do it. Through this work we have come to value:

- ***Individuals and interactions*** *over processes and tools*

- ***Working software*** *over comprehensive documentation*

- ***Customer collaboration*** *over contract negotiation*

- ***Responding to change*** *over following a plan*

That is, while there is value in the items on the right, we value the items on the left more.

Core Values of the Agile Manifesto

The four core values stated in the Agile Manifesto are explained as follows:

Individuals and interactions over processes and tools
<u>While there is value in processes and tools, we value individuals and interactions more.</u>

The single-minded focus on processes and tools restricts new ideas and makes it harder for people to conform to processes. Agile teams strive to eliminate unproductive and time-consuming processes to maximize the amount of work not done.

This principle <u>does not mean</u> that you should throw away any processes or tools that promote collaboration, increase technical agility, or improve the performance of your engineers. Collaboration tools like Slack, Skype for Business, etc. enable an open and collaborative team environment and must be encouraged. Any rigid processes that impede the velocity and agility of the team should be eliminated.

Working software over comprehensive documentation
<u>While there is value in the documentation, we value working software more.</u>

Agile teams focus on delivering working software frequently instead of creating comprehensive documentation upfront. With Agile, we strongly believe that it is not possible to know all the requirements and plans upfront. Agile methods support minimal ***just-in-time documentation*** that adds value.

The idea is to move away from the extensive documentation needs with the traditional plan-driven development approach.

Customer collaboration over contract negotiation

While there is value in contract negotiation, we value customer collaboration more.

Agile encourages collaboration, early feedback, and an environment of mutual trust between customers and the development team.

Agile teams embrace change and iterate on product features in close collaboration with customers instead of adhering to a binding upfront contract or a written agreement.

To exemplify this core value, you should understand your customer's behaviors, problems, goals, and motivations. You should build your product in close coordination with your customer and seek their early feedback.

Since the information available at the start of any initiative is minimal, you should not create upfront contracts or take important decisions until the **last responsible moment (LRM)**. LRM is a strategy of not making a premature decision, delaying commitment, and keeping the options open until the cost of not making a decision becomes greater than the cost of making a decision.

Responding to change over following a plan
While there is value in following a plan, we value responding to change more.

Agile teams do not follow a rigid, upfront plan. Instead, they quickly respond to change and deliver a valuable product. Any changes to completed work require only minimal rework since work is delivered in time-boxed iterations.

Exercise 1: Test your knowledge

- What is the Agile Manifesto?
- What does each of the four values in the Agile Manifesto mean to you?

Exercise 2: Brainstorming

Brainstorm with your team and list down all day-to-day activities that exemplify the values contained in the Agile Manifesto?

Learn all about Agile Scrum with my other bestselling book, The Basics Of Scrum – A Simple Handbook to the Most Popular Agile Scrum Framework.

Chapter 3 – The Agile Principles

"The impression that 'our problems are different' is a common disease that afflicts management the world over. They are different, to be sure, but the principles that will help to improve the quality of product and service are universal in nature."
—W. Edwards Deming

In this chapter, we will learn the 12 Agile Principles that form the foundation for being agile. The following principles are based on the Agile Manifesto.

Agile Principle 1: Our highest priority is to satisfy the customer through early and continuous delivery of valuable software.

What does this principle mean? The phrase ***"our highest priority"*** signifies that the entire product team should know their priorities and should work on the highest priority items first. The highest priority for the product team is to "*satisfy the customer*" such that the product meets the needs of the customer.

The phrase "*early and continuous delivery of valuable software*" implies that the work completed during the iteration must be demonstrated to the customers as soon as it meets the 'Definition of Done' to get their early feedback. Moreover, the team must strive to deliver valuable software to the customers at the end of each time-bound iteration.

Agile Principle 2: Welcome changing requirements, even late in development. Agile processes harness change for the customer's competitive advantage.

This principle focuses on embracing change. The phrase "**welcome changing requirements**" signifies the importance of accepting revised business priorities. The phrase "**even late in development**" signifies that changes should be welcomed irrespective of the time and effort the team has already invested to develop a feature. It's hard not to get defensive! But, think from your customer's perspective and understand the business value or the key drivers of the change.

"Intelligence is the ability to adapt to change."
– Stephen Hawking

Consider a scenario where an Agile team is developing a new feature to build a reporting suite. Four weeks before the scheduled release date, customers or product stakeholders decide to leverage a third-party vendor for their reporting needs. The product owner reprioritizes the work for the Agile team to integrate with the third-party product. Though this change came in quite late in development, the team should welcome the change and understand the rationale behind the decision.

In a practical world, customers or product owners would be quite cautious to make such a change and would ensure that the development team clearly understands the business benefits that led to this decision. As rightly stated in this principle, **"Agile processes harness change for the customer's competitive advantage."**

"Your life does not get better by chance; it gets better by change."
- Jim Rohn

Agile Principle 3: Deliver working software frequently, from a couple of weeks to a couple of months, with a preference to the shorter timescale.

Let's understand what this principle means. The phrase, "**deliver working software**" means that the Agile development team should aim to deliver a potentially shippable product increment or in other words, high-quality production-ready work, at the end of each iteration.

The remaining verbiage in the principle focuses on the delivery **frequency**. The principle signifies that the team should target to deliver working software frequently, preferably, after every couple of weeks. The shorter the delivery timescale, the more incremental development happens with the lesser cost of change.

Agile Principle 4: Business people and developers must work together daily throughout the project.

This principle focuses on **collaboration** between the business and the development team. The phrase "**must work together daily**" reminds us that Agile development teams must interact with the business or product sponsors daily throughout the work execution.

> *"Individual commitment to a group effort – that is what makes a teamwork, a company work, a society work, a civilization work."*
> *- Vince Lombardi*

Agile Principle 5: Build projects around motivated individuals. Give them the environment and support they need, and trust them to get the job done.

What does this principle mean? The phrase, **"build around motivated individuals"** emphasizes the importance of having motivated people on the team. Inspired people, who want to make a difference in this world, increase the overall team's efficiency.

> *"Find people who share your values, and you'll conquer the world together."*
> *—John Ratzenberger*

"Give them the environment and support they need" – this phrase means that agile leaders should provide the necessary infrastructure and support that development teams need to continuously integrate and deploy their changes.

The other important aspect of this principle is "**trust**". The principle states that agile leaders must trust the motivated agile team to incrementally and iteratively deliver valuable software to customers.

Agile Principle 6: The most efficient and effective method of conveying information to and within a development team is a face-to-face conversation.

This principle is all about the **face-to-face conversation**. Agile leaders, product sponsors, and business stakeholders must meet with the development team in-person regularly. Face-to-face conversations boost creativity, credibility, trust, and collaboration as people better understand feelings and reactions via body language and expressions. Face-to-face conversations also promote friendliness and build relationships.

Often, face-to-face conversations are constrained by the geographical presence of the development team. In such scenarios, the business or the product team should plan to travel and meet the development team in-person at regular intervals or at least have video conversations with the team frequently. Similarly, for communications within the development team, the principle recommends face-to-face conversations.

Agile Principle 7: Working software is the primary measure of progress.

This principle focuses on "**working software**". The Agile development team must deliver high-quality work at the end of each iteration that can be released on-demand to end-users or customers of the product. The principle states that working software is the **primary success measure**. Other metrics such as productivity, committed vs actual work, and burndown charts are secondary.

Agile Principle 8: Agile processes promote sustainable development. The sponsors, developers, and users should be able to maintain a constant pace indefinitely.

What does this principle mean? The phrase "**sustainable development**" means that work is developed at a **constant pace** that can be sustained **indefinitely** without overburdening a development team. The sponsors, developers, and users should be able to maintain a constant pace indefinitely.

> *"It does not matter how slowly you go as long as you do not stop."*
> *– Confucius*

Agile Principle 9: Continuous attention to technical excellence and good design enhances agility.

The principle states that agile leaders, developers, and the product team must continuously seek **technical excellence and emergent design** to enhance agility. Building an architectural runway or the infrastructure required by the team to continuously integrate and deploy code leads to technical excellence. Agile teams keep the design options flexible as long as possible during development and explore multiple design solutions to arrive at the best design choice. This approach provides maximum flexibility and innovation.

> *"In an agile project, technical excellence is measured by both capacity to deliver customer value today and create an adaptable product for tomorrow."*
> *- Jim Highsmith*

Agile Principle 10: Simplicity--the art of maximizing the amount of work not done--is essential.

The developers, product sponsors, and agile leaders must identify things that do not add value or in other words, must **simplify things by maximizing the amount of work not done.**

> *"A designer knows he has achieved perfection not when there is nothing left to add, but when there is, nothing left to take away."*
> *– Antoine de Saint-Exupery*

Agile Principle 11: The best architectures, requirements, and designs emerge from self-organizing teams.

This principle is all about **self-organizing teams**. The product architecture, design, and features emerge from mature self-organizing teams who can freely make decisions and remove temporary blockers on their own. If developers are free to make decisions, they tend to be more accountable, innovative, and collaborative. Such an environment is best suited for emergent design and iterative development.

> *"A self-organizing team has authority over its work and the process it uses."*
> - *Mike Cohn*

Agile Principle 12: At regular intervals, the team reflects on how to become more effective, then tunes and adjusts its behavior accordingly.

This principle focuses on **inspect and adapt**. The phrase "**at regular intervals**" signifies the importance of setting up a regular cadence to inspect and improve. Agile frameworks recommend regular practices such as product demo and retrospectives to continuously improve the process iteratively.

> *"Continuous improvement is better than delayed perfection."*
> - *Mark Twain*

Exercise 1: Test your knowledge

- What do these principles mean to you?
- Explain Agile Principle #8 to your colleague and/or friend.

Exercise 2: Brainstorming

- Brainstorm with your team, evaluate your team's agile maturity against these 12 principles and write down three action items that you will take to improve your team's agile maturity.
- List down three things that you will change in your behavior to be more agile.

Also, read my article, "What are the Agile Principles?", on Medium and my website: https://authoraditiagarwal.com

Chapter 4 – Agile Frameworks

"In preparing for battles I have always found that plans are useless, but planning is indispensable"
- *Dwight Eisenhower*

This chapter covers a brief introduction of different Agile frameworks that are used by various organizations. An Agile framework is defined as a specific approach to software development based on the Agile Manifesto.

The most popular Agile methodologies are listed as follows:

- Scrum
- Extreme Programming (XP)
- Feature-Driven Development (FDD)
- Dynamic Systems Development Method (DSDM)

- The Crystal Method

Unfortunately, there is no one-size-fits-all way to adopt Agile development. Based on your organization's size and structure, you may choose the framework that works the best for your organization.

Scrum

Scrum is an iterative or incremental process framework to build **complex** products of the **highest possible value**.

Scrum was developed to solve problems with the traditional plan-based methodology such as the mismatch between requirements and the implemented product, late customer feedback, low team morale, rework, high cost of change, and slow time to market.

In Scrum, the team always works on the highest priority items first. The work is performed in short, time-boxed **iterations or sprints**. Each iteration begins when the team aligns on a subset of the highest priority items that it can complete in that iteration. Each iteration ends when the team has delivered a **potentially shippable product increment** of the product. The team delivers value to the customer at the end of each iteration or a time-boxed cycle.

Scrum prescribes three **roles** - Product Owner, Scrum Master, and the Development Team. A **Product Owner** decides what needs to be built and in what order. A **Scrum Master** acts as a servant leader, removes impediments, and coaches the team to follow Agile principles. A **Development Team** is a group of self-organizing individuals who develop a high-quality product, collaborate with the product owner, and participate in scrum ceremonies.

Besides specific roles, Scrum prescribes **ceremonies** that must be conducted on regular cadence each iteration or sprint such as Backlog Refinement, Sprint Planning, Daily Stand-up, Sprint Review, and Sprint Retrospective.

The **Backlog Refinement** or Backlog Grooming is a ceremony to create, refine, estimate, and prioritize work. This ceremony is usually conducted a few days before the start of the upcoming sprint.

Sprint Planning takes place at the beginning of each Sprint. During Sprint Planning, the team discusses prioritized, refined, and ready user stories in the product backlog. The Scrum Master shares available team capacity for the sprint after considering planned time-off by the development team. Prioritized user stories are then added to the sprint backlog until the team capacity runs out. The team commits to complete user stories in the sprint backlog and splits each committed user story into tasks. The team then estimates these tasks in terms of hours and assign these to themselves.

The **daily stand-up** is a 15-minute activity that takes place each day of the Sprint, at the same time. During this ceremony, each team member speaks to below three questions:

- What did I do yesterday?
- What will I do today?
- What are the impediments that prevent me to make progress?

It is recommended to stand-up during this ceremony to keep it short. If meetings can stay short and on-topic, then standing up may not be necessary. The intent is <u>not to provide a status update to the Scrum Master</u>.

Sprint Review is an <u>inspect and adapt</u> activity in which the stakeholders review the completed work at the end of each Sprint. In this ceremony, the team provides a **demo of the product** with new features or work that was completed in the Sprint.

This ceremony provides an opportunity for the team to seek early **feedback** from the stakeholders and gain **visibility** of their work.

Sprint Retrospective is the second **'inspect and adapt'** ceremony that happens at the end of each Sprint. During this meeting, the entire team comes together and discusses what worked best, what went wrong, and what can be done to improve in the upcoming iteration.

Learn all about Agile Scrum with my other bestselling book, The Basics Of Scrum – A Simple Handbook to the Most Popular Agile Scrum Framework.

Extreme Programming (XP)

Extreme Programming (XP) is one of several popular Agile frameworks that emphasize building high-quality software, adapting to changing business needs, empowering developers, test-driven development, automated testing, iterative development, continuous integration, and pair-programming.

In Extreme Programming (XP), work is performed in short, time-boxed iterations at a sustainable pace. The iterations in XP are typically 1-2 weeks long as compared to 2-4 weeks in Scrum. XP practices are quite similar to those of Scrum.

Extreme Programming (XP) framework emphasizes teamwork, collaboration, simplicity, feedback, respect, and courage, along with a set of simple rules.

Let's take a look at the XP rules below:

- User stories are written.
- Release planning creates the release schedule.
- Make frequent small releases.
- The project is divided into iterations.
- Iteration planning starts with each iteration.
- Give the team a dedicated open workspace.
- Set a sustainable pace.
- A stand-up meeting starts each day.
- The project velocity is measured.
- Move people around.
- Fix XP when it breaks.
- Simplicity
- Choose a system metaphor.
- Use CRC cards for design sessions.
- Create spike solutions to reduce risk.
- No functionality is added early.

- Refactor whenever and wherever possible.
- The customer is always available.
- Code must be written to agreed standards.
- Code the unit test first.
- All production code is pair-programmed.
- Only one pair integrates code at a time.
- Integrate often
- Set up a dedicated integration computer.
- Use collective ownership.
- All code must have unit tests.
- Code must pass all unit tests before it can be released.
- When a bug is found, tests are created.
- Acceptance tests are run often, and the score is published.

These rules are based on Extreme Programming (XP) values below:

- Simplicity
- Communication
- Feedback
- Respect
- Courage

Feature-Driven Development

Feature-Driven Development (FDD), developed by **Jeff De Luca**, is one of the Agile frameworks that is heavily focused on domain modeling and feature-driven incremental development. This methodology was designed to work with larger teams, though it is said to work for smaller teams as well.

The Feature-Driven Development (FDD) framework encourages organizations or large teams to follow a simple **five-step development process** as follows:

- Develop an Overall Model
- Build a Features List
- Plan by Feature
- Design by Feature
- Build by Feature

Develop an Overall Model
Building an initial object model is an iterative and collaborative activity at the start of a project. The idea is to have a shared understanding of the problem at the start. The object model is a living document that is updated iteratively throughout the project.

Build a Features List
FDD defines Features as a small, client-valued function expressed in the form:
<action><result><object>

Example:
Add a login button to the home page.

A Feature in FDD is similar to a User Story in Scrum. A Feature typically takes 1-3 days to complete. And, it should never take more than 10 days to complete. FDD organizes its Features into a three-level hierarchy or the Features List.

Plan by Feature
The team sequences Features by their relative business value, technical risk, and dependencies. The team then selects Features to complete during the iteration. Unlike Scrum, the team assigns individual developers to specific domain classes.

Design by Feature (DBF)
The assigned lead developer runs a series of iterations with a duration ranging from a few days to two weeks. Unlike Scrum, the duration of the iteration or sprint is not constant here. The lead developer forms a feature team for each iteration. The feature team typically comprises of 3-5 people who are assigned class owners for development in that iteration. The

lead developer then facilitates the analysis and design of features in that iteration.

Build by Feature (BFD)
The team starts to write code, execute unit tests, and feature-level tests to complete features in the iteration. FDD does not prescribe if tests are written before or after writing the code.

This five-step process allows for rapid development by leveraging pre-defined development standards and by organizing work around discrete "feature" projects.

Dynamic Systems Development Method (DSDM)

DSDM was introduced in 1994 to replace the unstructured Rapid Application Development (RAD) framework. DSDM is an Agile framework that covers the entire lifecycle of a project and is often used in conjunction with traditional methods or other Agile frameworks. DSDM fully embraces the Agile Manifesto.

In the traditional plan-driven approach, the project scope is fixed whereas time and cost may vary. DSDM's approach has fixed time, cost, and quality, while project scope may vary as needed.

The eight principles of the Dynamic Systems Development Method (DSDM) are listed as follows:

- Focus on the business need
- Deliver on time
- Collaborate
- Never compromise quality
- Build incrementally from firm foundations
- Develop interactively
- Communicate continuously and clearly
- Demonstrate control

DSDM prescribes the use of several proven practices including:

- Facilitated Workshops
- Modeling and Iterative Development
- MoSCoW Prioritization
- Time Boxing

Crystal

Crystal was developed by **Alistair Cockburn** for IBM in 1991. Per Cockburn, "*Crystal is a family of human-powered, adaptive, ultra-light, 'stretch-to-fit' software development methodologies.*"

The Crystal family is a collection of Agile methodologies that focus on people interactions and business priorities. Crystal does not prescribe any development tools and methods to start with; the same is determined based on business and technical needs.

The Crystal family of methodologies consists of the following variants: Crystal Clear, Crystal Yellow, Crystal Orange, Crystal Orange Web, Crystal Red, Crystal Maroon, Crystal Diamond, and Crystal Sapphire. The team size, environment, and criticality determine the methodology to be used – ranging from Crystal Clear (which is used for small, co-located teams up to 6 people) to Crystal Sapphire (which is used in large projects with potential risk to human life).

Crystal recommends below practices that are crucial for successful implementation of the Crystal approach:

- Iterative and Incremental development
- Active user involvement
- Delivering on commitments

With this, you have learned popular Agile frameworks for software development. Out of all these, Scrum and Extreme Programming (XP) are the more popular ones.

Exercise 1: Test your knowledge

- What Agile frameworks did you learn with this chapter?

- When will you choose Scrum vs XP?

Exercise 2: Brainstorming

- Brainstorm with your team and explore which Agile framework works the best for your organization.

*If you learned something from this book, please submit your **honest review** on Amazon.*

Chapter 5 – Scaling Agile

"Learn from yesterday, live for today, hope for tomorrow. The important thing is not to stop questioning."
- *Albert Einstein*

When leaders want to scale agile across the enterprise, they often fail because agile frameworks that worked well for small teams do not scale well for larger programs. Large programs with several teams need consistent processes and practices along with executive sponsorship to solve scaling problems.

For scaling agile across the enterprise, executive leaders must be on-board since the adoption of a scaling agile framework will need a significant amount of investment. People will need to be trained and certified to implement the framework. Since the transition is a significant business commitment, organizations should perform a self-assessment and explore if they have reached the tipping point.

Some of the questions that leaders may consider are listed below:

- Is the organization struggling to sustain or compete with ever-changing market conditions, emerging technology trends, and increased competition?

- Are you able to achieve business outcomes?

- Are your practices and processes still beneficial?

- Do you have a systematic way to make decisions and resolve conflicts?

- Are you delivering end-to-end value to your customers?

- Do you need to better manage dependencies across systems or teams to avoid unnecessary delays?

- Do you lack trust and transparency between stakeholders and teams?

- Are people motivated and engaged? Are they over-burdened?

- Will existing agile teams be able to perform in a scaled environment?

- What's the time to market? Can you deliver high-quality products frequently to your customers?

- Is the overall system, portfolio, or the enterprise agile?

- Do you have a systematic approach to measure predictability across teams?

- Have you accumulated technical debt?

- Have you noticed Agile anti-patterns within your teams? Do your teams practice Agile in name only? Do they operate like Zombie Scrum teams?

- Do you have large, complex systems that are difficult to manage? What is the average size and complexity of your teams and products?

- Do you want to proactively drive change to the organization and achieve better outcomes?

- What benefits would "Scaled Agile" bring to your organization?

Conducting research and performing self-assessment will help you to gain alignment and scale agile to your enterprise.

This chapter introduces scaled Agile frameworks that organizations, portfolios, and teams embrace to scale agile to the enterprise. The three most popular scaled Agile frameworks are listed as follows:

- Scaled Agile Framework (SAFe)
- Large Scale Scrum (LeSS)
- Disciplined Agile Delivery (DaD)

Scaled Agile Framework (SAFe)

Founded by **Dean Leffingwell**, Scaled Agile Framework (SAFe) is a knowledge base of proven, integrated principles, practices, and competencies for **Lean**, **Agile**, and **DevOps**.

SAFe provides a structure to effectively plan at the **team**, **program**, or **portfolio** level.

Cross-functional Agile teams leverage Scrum, Kanban, or Extreme Programming (XP) to build software iteratively and incrementally. Although teams iterate on a regular cadence, it is tough for a single team of 5-11 people to deliver end-to-end business value for complex systems across different technology platforms.

Thus, agile teams operate within an **Agile Release Train** or **ART** which is essentially a team of agile teams with around 50-125 people. ART provides a common structure with shared principles at a program level such that agile teams can plan together, collaborate better, develop on cadence, and release on-demand. The Scaled Agile Framework defines unique roles needed for successful ART execution such as **Release Train Engineer**, Program Managers, System Architects, etc.

To build large and complex solutions that need hundreds of people, SAFe proposes organizing multiple ARTs and teams into a **Solution Train**. The Solution Train manages the large-scale development and aligns ARTs with a shared mission, vision, and roadmap. It also provides additional roles, events, and artifacts needed to build solution capabilities.

At a portfolio level, **value streams** represent the steps required to implement large-scale solutions or capabilities that provide end-to-end value to customers. SAFe portfolios are organized around value streams to visualize the flow of work from the start to the finish. They prioritize work based on **Strategic Themes**, **Portfolio Vision**, and **Portfolio Backlog**.

Today, SAFe is adopted by around 70% of the Fortune 100 companies. More people are being trained and certified through different role-based certifications every year.

SAFe supports multiple **configurations**:
- Essential SAFe
- Large Solution SAFe
- Portfolio SAFe
- Full SAFe

Essential SAFe is the most simple and fundamental building block for all SAFe configurations and includes the Agile Release Train (ART) and teams. **Large Solution SAFe** supports the development of large, complex systems and is comprised of the Solution Train, Agile Release Trains, and teams. **The Portfolio SAFe** configuration enables business agility for an organization and provides principles and practices for portfolio vision, strategy, operations, and governance.

Full SAFe is the most comprehensive configuration needed for business agility.

The core values of SAFe are as follows:
- Alignment
- Built-in quality
- Transparency
- Program Execution

Enterprises cannot embrace change without alignment. **Alignment** is needed at all levels, starting from strategic themes, portfolio vision, solution backlog, and program backlog, to the product backlog, sprint goals, etc.

Built-in quality is a foundational need during software development. Without it, organizations will accumulate technical debt and will waste their effort in rework. As Deming rightly said:

"Inspection does not improve the quality, nor guarantee quality. Inspection is too late. The quality, good or bad, is already in the product. Quality cannot be inspected into a product or service; it must be built into it."
- W. Edwards Deming

Transparency and trust play a critical role in building complex systems. With clear visibility into PI Objectives, Program Backlog, and other artifacts, teams build mutual trust. Everyone can view the upcoming initiatives, product roadmap, team's velocity, and work-in-progress items at any given point in time.

Program Execution is another core value of the SAFe framework. Teams are organized into Agile Release Trains and Agile teams to execute work and deliver value.

The nine underlying principles of SAFe are derived from the **core principles** of Agile, Lean, DevOps. These fundamental principles lay the foundation for SAFe practices.

- Take an economic view
- Apply systems thinking
- Assume variability; preserve options
- Build incrementally with fast, integrated learning cycles
- Base milestones on the objective evaluation of working systems
- Visualize and limit WIP, reduce batch sizes, and manage queue lengths
- Apply cadence, synchronize with cross-domain planning

- Unlock the intrinsic motivation of knowledge workers
- Decentralize decision-making
- Organize around value

Take an economic view
This principle means that leaders and teams should understand the economic impact of their decisions. They should prioritize or sequence work to minimize the cost of delay and to ensure that the highest value is delivered in the shortest lead time, based on the Weighted Shortest Job First (WSJF).

Apply Systems Thinking
This principle depicts three primary aspects of systems thinking:

- The Solution itself is a System
- The Enterprise building the System is a System too
- Optimize the full Value Stream

Assume variability; preserve options
This principle is to manage variability and to preserve options with a set-based design to build great solutions. In the Set-Based Design (SBD) or Set-Based Concurrent Engineering (SBCE) approach, developers start with multiple choices of design and then eliminate weaker options over-time before they narrow

down on the final design. This way, options remain open for as much time as possible.

Build incrementally with fast, integrated learning cycles

This principle encourages incremental development in a series for short timeboxes, integration points, or iterations. The knowledge gathered after each iteration is leveraged to assess technical feasibility, improve solution design, or to pivot to an alternate design.

Base milestones on the objective evaluation of working systems

According to this principle, the system should be measured and evaluated frequently throughout the development lifecycle at the end of every iteration or milestone.

Visualize and limit WIP, reduce batch sizes, and manage queue lengths

The three ways to achieve continuous flow are:

- Visualize and limit WIP
- Reduce the batch sizes of work items
- Manage queue lengths

Having a large WIP (work in progress) promotes context-switching, decreases productivity, and increases wait time. Thus, the flow and the current WIP should be visible to all stakeholders via a Kanban Board. Then, the team should continually adjust their WIP to improve the flow.

Teams should also decrease the batch sizes of the work, in other words, write smaller user stories. Small batch sizes move through the flow quickly with less variability.

The third method to improve flow is to reduce the queue length. The larger the backlog, the longer the wait time is.

Apply cadence, synchronize with cross-domain planning

This principle focuses on cadence, synchronization, and cross-domain planning that are critical to effective solution development. Cadence is the rhythm of events or scheduled integration points for cross-domain planning. One of the examples is to schedule events such as PI Planning, System Demos, ART Sync, and regular scrum ceremonies with a predictable cadence for the entire year such that these events become a routine for the team and the team can focus on developing solutions.

Synchronization allows multiple events to be integrated at the same time. The Innovation and

Planning (IP) iteration enables multiple agile teams to synchronize their work.

Unlock the intrinsic motivation of knowledge workers

Leaders should provide autonomy to encourage self-organizing teams. They should unite the team with a common purpose, mission, and a strong vision so that the team can make decisions, collaborate effectively, be productive, and learn new skills.

Decentralize decision-making

Decentralized decision-making reduces delays in decision-making, empowers people, and improves the overall product development flow. Not all decisions should be decentralized. If decisions are infrequent, long-lasting, and provide significant economies of scale, then they should stay centralized. On the other hand, if decisions are frequent, time-critical, and need local context, then they should be decentralized.

Organize around value

People and resources should be organized into value streams to deliver quickly. This way, the enterprise will be able to learn faster, embrace change, and innovate continually.

A value stream represents a series of steps to implement solutions that provide a continuous flow of value to customers. A value stream can be realized by either a single Agile Release Train (ART) or multiple ARTs in a Solution Train. There could also be multiple value streams that can be realized by a single ART. Enterprises that can organize around value streams have business agility.

You may refer to case studies, glossary, resources, training, blogs, and much more on www.scaledagileframework.com and www.scaledagile.com

Scaled Agile Framework and SAFe are trademarks of © **Scaled Agile, Inc**.

Large-Scale Scrum (LeSS)

Founded by **Bas Vodde** and **Craig Larman**, the Large-Scale Scrum framework scales the Scrum framework to multiple teams working on the same product. In LeSS, there's only one Product Backlog, one Product Owner, one Scrum Master, one Definition of Done, and one Potentially Shippable Product Increment.

The regular Scrum ceremonies - Sprint Planning, Backlog Refinement, Sprint Review, and Sprint Retrospective, are conducted for all of the teams together.

LeSS Framework supports a "**multi-team Scrum**" rather than "**multiple Scrum teams**". With "multiple scrum teams", each team has a separate Product Owner but a common product backlog as all teams work on the same product. In this approach, multiple Product Owners will need to collaborate and align on product priorities for the iteration. In the "multi-team Scrum" setting, there's a single Product Owner who works with multiple cross-functional teams working on the same product.

There are two types of LeSS - **Basic LeSS** and **LeSS Huge**. Basic LeSS applies to 2-8 small teams developing the same product. LeSS Huge is used for more than eight teams.

The principles of the LeSS framework are:

- Large-Scale Scrum is Scrum
- Systems Thinking
- Lean Thinking
- Empirical Process Control
- Queueing Theory
- Transparency
- More with LeSS
- Whole Product Focus
- Customer-Centric
- Continuous Improvement towards Perfection

Large-Scale Scrum is Scrum
This principle signifies that Large-Scale Scrum (LeSS) is essentially scaling the Scrum framework and applying its principles in a multi-team context.

Systems Thinking
LeSS emphasizes understanding and optimizing the whole system rather than individual products or features. The focus is to reduce the lead time of the overall flow from concept to cash, not individual steps.

Lean Thinking
LeSS encourages lean thinking. Lean managers practice respect for people, continuous improvement, and 'Gemba' (observing the workspace) to pursue perfection. The goal of Lean thinking is to deliver the best quality and value in the shortest sustainable lead-time.

Empirical Process Control
Empirical process control is a core Scrum principle. It encourages transparency, self-organizing teams, and the inspect-adapt cycle so that teams can inspect their existing processes and take actionable steps for continuous improvement.

Queueing Theory
This LeSS principle stresses the importance to understand the queueing theory – the mathematical analysis of how work items move across the system with queues, and to manage queue sizes, work in progress (WIP) limits, context-switching, and variability.

LeSS supports the implications of queueing theory. Example queues in software development are features waiting to be prioritized, code waiting to be tested, components waiting to be integrated, and so on.

Transparency
Without transparency, it is hard to reduce cycle time, queue lengths, or the WIP limit. The inspect and adapt cycle, with the help of product demos and team retrospectives, is critical for continuous improvement. By having an aligned "Definition of Ready" and "Definition of Done", you are being transparent with your product stakeholders.

More with LeSS
LeSS framework does not add additional roles, processes, ceremonies, artifacts, etc. to keep it simple for organizations to adopt the same. More roles lead to less responsible teams, more processes lead to less ownership, and more artifacts lead to less customer focus.

Whole-product Focus
With LeSS, there is one Product Backlog, one Product Owner, one Sprint, and one potentially shippable product increment. This principle focuses on developing the whole product rather than standalone parts of a system. Teams who finished building their components are not done until they have integrated with the whole.

Customer-Centric
In large groups with multiple teams, people often write code without understanding customer value. With LeSS, the focus is on feature teams rather than component teams that deliver end-to-end customer-centric features. The single Product Owner shared by all teams ensures that the overall system is delivering maximum customer value.

Continuous Improvement towards Perfection
This principle signifies the importance of continuous improvement and creating a defect-free product. In Large-Scale Scrum (LeSS), there are no change forum or change request approvers since change is continuous through experimentation and improvement.

Continuous improvement towards perfection is also a pillar in Lean thinking originated from the Toyota Way.

You may learn more about the Large-Scale Scrum (LeSS) framework here: https://less.works/less/framework/index.html

Disciplined Agile Delivery (DaD) or Disciplined Agile (DA)

Disciplined Agile Delivery (DaD) or now renamed as Disciplined Agile (DA) toolkit is a hybrid approach that extends strategies from Scrum, Extreme Programming, Kanban, and other Agile and Lean methodologies to deliver large, complex systems.

This toolkit provides a solid foundation to large organizations for business agility and highlights the scalable people-first approach, enterprise-thinking, and the end-to-end delivery lifecycle.

Disciplined Agile Delivery (DAD) was originally developed by IBM in 2009. The 1.0 version was released in June 2012 with the publication of the book, Disciplined Agile Delivery. The ownership of DAD passed on to the Disciplined Agile Consortium in October 2012. The Disciplined Agile 2.x toolkit was released in August 2015 and the Disciplined Agile 3.x toolkit was released in August 2017. The latest version is the Disciplined Agile 5.x toolkit which was released in May 2020 along with the revised version of the book, Choose Your WoW!

The PMI Disciplined Agile (DA) toolkit comprises of 4 layers as below:

- Foundation
- Disciplined DevOps
- Value Streams
- Disciplined Agile Enterprise (DAE)

Foundation
This layer lays out principles, promises, and guidelines of the Disciplined Agile mindset with concepts from Agile, Lean, PMBOK Guide, DevOps, Traditional Waterfall, Unified Process (UP), Agile Modeling (AM), Scaled Agile Framework (SAFe), and more.
The PMI Disciplined Agile (DA) toolkit principles are:

- Delight customers
- Be awesome
- Context counts
- Be pragmatic
- Choice is good
- Optimize flow
- Organize around products/services
- Enterprise awareness

Delight customers
Being customer-centric is at the heart of this toolkit. This principle encourages teams to build with users in mind, collaborate, seek early feedback, embrace change, and go above and beyond to delight customers.

Be Awesome
Do the best you can each day and be awesome. This principle encourages engaged individuals to perform their best, build awesome teams, and relentlessly improve towards perfection.

Motivated individuals who are open, honest, and reliable build awesome teams that collaborate, experiment, learn, improve, and deliver better outcomes.

Context counts
Each organization, portfolio, program, and team operate in their unique context. Each group should carefully select their way of working (WoW) based on their current context.

Be pragmatic
This principle states that we should be pragmatic and adopt the methodology that makes the most sense to our context. One should be willing to embrace Agile, Lean, or even traditional Waterfall methodology if that works best for their team.

Choice is good
The DA toolkit offers choices to teams so they can select the process or methodology that works best for them with process goal diagrams. To make these choices, teams need to understand each option and the trade-offs associated with each. Better choices lead teams to better outcomes.

Optimize flow
This principle focuses on optimizing the end-to-end workflow. For that, we need to organize around value streams, visualize the overall flow, limit Work in Progress (WIP), deliver continuously at a sustainable pace, eliminate waste, experiment, improve continuously, and measure what matters.

Organize around products/services
Rather than organizing teams around business units or job functions such as marketing, sales, finance, project management, etc., we should create cross-functional teams and organize around products/services to optimize the end-to-end flow or the value stream.

Enterprise awareness
This is one of the core principles of the Disciplined Agile toolkit. DA teams break their silos and work closely with enterprise systems, architects, and teams. They adopt Enterprise

Architecture, Frameworks, Templates, Guidelines, Practices, Governance, and Infrastructure.

Disciplined DevOps
This layer streamlines processes for Disciplined Agile (DA) teams around DevOps including Security, Data Management, Release Management, IT Operations, Business Operations, Support, and more.

Value Streams
This layer provides process areas to define value streams and organize work around value streams such as Portfolio Management, Product Management, Program Management, Governance, Marketing, Sales, Strategy, etc.

Disciplined Agile Enterprise (DAE)
This layer provides additional process areas that enable any organization to respond and pivot quickly to changes in the marketplace. These process areas include Enterprise Architecture, Finance, Legal, People Management, Asset Management, and more.

You may read more about Disciplined Agile here: https://www.pmi.org/disciplined-agile

Exercise 1: Test your knowledge

- What are the principles of the Scaled Agile Framework (SAFe)?
- What are the principles of Large-Scale Scrum (LeSS)?
- What are the principles of Disciplined Agile (DA)?

Exercise 2: Brainstorming

Brainstorm with your colleagues and evaluate the scaled Agile framework that best suits your enterprise or portfolio.

Learn all about Agile Scrum with my other bestselling book, The Basics Of Scrum – A Simple Handbook to the Most Popular Agile Scrum Framework.

Chapter 6 – What is Lean?

"Introducing a radical change is harder than incrementally improving an existing one."
- David J. Anderson

This chapter introduces you to concepts, principles, and history of the Lean methodology.

What Is the Lean Methodology?

Lean is a customer-centric methodology that focuses on **respect for people, continuous improvement**, **maximizing customer value**, and **eliminating waste**.

Lean defines value from the customer's perspective, continuously improves how value is delivered, and eliminates wasteful resources that do not contribute to the value goal. Rather than optimizing each product on its own, Lean thinking encourages to **optimize the flow of**

work through **value streams** across technologies, departments, and products. Lean has become very popular as a way of thinking in many enterprises.

The History of Lean

The Lean Methodology originated from the Toyota Production System in the 1950s. After World War II, **Kiichiro Toyoda** and **Taiichi Ohno** from Toyota revisited the manufacturing techniques of Henry Ford and the statistical quality control processes of Edwards Deming to set the foundation for the **Toyota Production System (TPS).**

The Toyota Production System shifted the focus from improving individual products or machines to optimizing across the entire value stream. This system was established based on two major concepts – **Jidoka** and **Just-in-Time**. The term 'Jidoka' means '**automation with human intelligence**' or '**autonomation**'. With Jidoka, the equipment stops when a problem arises which forces workers to solve the problem to start the production line. The '**Just-in-Time**' concept is to produce only what is needed, when it is needed, and in quantities needed.

Lean will never be something you _do_, it is something you _become._ To become Lean, the organization's culture must change and focus on respect for people. In 2007, James P. Womack described how Toyota managers show **respect for people** by following a problem-solving process that requires them to challenge their employees, seek their thoughts, and speak to them about the best solution.

Here's the problem-solving process laid out by J. P. Womack:

- Managers begin by "taking Gemba walks" or in other words, walking around the workplace to see what's happening. They ask their employees what the problem is.
- They challenge their employees' responses and question them on their understanding of the problem to find out what the real problem is.
- Then they ask what is causing the problem and what are the root causes of the problem.
- Managers ask employees to propose a solution and then question why they proposed one solution over the other. This way, managers gather alternate solutions and supporting data for each.

- Managers also ask their people how they would know that problem is solved. In other words, managers ask employees' feedback on the success criteria for the proposed solution.
- Finally, when the solution is aligned, employees will implement the same.

By showing mutual respect, lean managers solve problems effectively and lead their organizations to perfection.

The 5 Traditional Lean Principles

The five traditional lean manufacturing principles that were first described in 1997 by James P. Womack and Daniel T. Jones, founders of <u>Lean Enterprise Institute</u>, are listed as below:

- Identify Value
- Map the Value Stream
- Create Flow
- Establish Pull
- Pursue Perfection

Identify Value
Lean teams strive to identify value from the standpoint of the end-user or customer.

Sometimes customers don't know what they want. Creating customer personas, analyzing customer behaviors, conducting customer interviews, researching demographic information, and studying analytics data are some of the wide-spread techniques used to uncover the value from a customer's perspective.

Some teams or products may not provide direct value to customers but are enhancing the overall organizational value. In such cases, the Lean team should consider their organization as their customer.

Map the Value Stream
The second core Lean principle is to map the value stream. A value stream is defined as a series of steps that an organization, portfolio, or team takes to deliver continuous value to its customers or end-users. Value stream mapping helps teams to understand how value flows end-to-end within their team, portfolio, or organization. It also enables teams to identify steps that do not create value or **waste**.

Lean specifies **7 types of waste** activities that can be categorized as **necessary waste** and **pure waste**. While necessary waste supports the value-adding activities and should be minimized, pure waste does not add any value and should be eliminated.

Create Flow
The third core Lean principle is to create and optimize the flow defined by the value stream map via continuous improvements to maximize the efficiencies of the value-adding steps and reducing bottlenecks or waste in the flow.

Some strategies to create a smooth flow include: breaking down the value map into smaller activities, observing the flow, distinguishing waste from value-adding activities, defining steps to reduce or eliminate waste, identifying improvements to tighten the value-adding steps, creating a cross-functional team, and providing growth opportunities.

Establish Pull
This Lean principle emphasizes the importance of a pull system. The concept of a simple pull system is to create value only when it is needed by the customer. In other words, **a pull system** allows for **Just-in-Time** development where products are created only on the customer demand and in the quantities needed.

Pursue Perfection
This core Lean principle emphasizes continuous improvement. The main goal for Lean teams is

to optimize the value-adding steps and reduce waste activities such that a smooth flow is established, and a state of perfection is reached.

One of the significant tools for continuous improvement is **Plan-Do-Check-Act (PDCA).** The PDCA model was popularized by Dr. W. Edwards Deming and is also known as **the Deming cycle**. The four sequential stages encourage to define the problem, implement a solution, measure results, and make recommendations for the next cycle. This cycle is often known as **Plan-Do-Check-Adjust** where the term **'adjust'** signifies continuous improvement.

The 7 Principles of Lean Software Development

The term **'Lean Software Development'** was conceptualized by Mary Poppendieck and Tom Poppendieck in 2003.

The Lean Software Development can be summarized by the 7 principles listed below:

- Eliminate waste
- Build quality in
- Create knowledge
- Deliver fast by managing the flow

- Defer commitment
- Respect people
- Optimize the whole

Eliminate Waste
Anything that a customer wouldn't pay for, is defined as waste in Lean thinking. Originally, **Taiichi Ohno**, from Toyota, identified 7 types of wastes as part of the Toyota Production System (TPS): Transportation, Inventory, Motion, Waiting, Overproduction, Over-processing, and Defects. They are often referred to by the acronym 'TIMWOOD'. In the 1990s, the 8th waste of 'Skills' was added to this list when the Toyota Production System was adopted in the west. Today, the 8 types of **manufacturing wastes** are commonly referred to as 'TIMWOODS'.

In **Lean Software Development**, different types of wastes are categorized as follows:

- Building the wrong feature or product
- Mismanaging the backlog
- Rework
- Unnecessarily complex solutions
- Extraneous cognitive load
- Psychological distress
- Context switching/multitasking

- Knowledge loss
- Ineffective communication

This principle focuses on eliminating anything that does not generate business value.

Build Quality In
This Lean principle for software development emphasizes the need to build high-quality work or products, automate complex, and repeatable processes that are prone to human error, integrate continuously with other pieces of work, refactor, and write clean code.

Create knowledge
This principle is focused on continuous learning and improvement by taking the time to hold retrospectives, cross-train team members, coach the team, create modular architecture, and build on emergent design.

Deliver fast by managing the flow
This Lean principle for software development signifies the importance to deliver fast by managing the flow of value. It encourages teams to continuously visualize and optimize flow. The flow efficiency for a team depends on the work-in-progress (WIP) for the team. As higher the WIP limit, the slower the flow of value is. Lean teams continuously strive to eliminate blockers, limit WIP, and increase their flow efficiency.

Defer commitment
This principle encourages organizations and teams to make irreversible decisions at the **last responsible moment** (LRM). This aligns with the Just-in-Time concept where organizations have the agility to make informed decisions based on the latest information.

Respect People
An enterprise that respects its people develops good leaders. Lean teams create an environment of mutual respect and trust to allow everyone to deliver the maximum value. Lean leaders nurture the skills of their people and trust them to get the work done.

Optimize the whole
Lean organizations optimize the whole system or the enterprise value stream. Value Streams are a series of steps, products, or systems that support a continuous flow of value to a customer. These value streams assist in identifying and addressing non-value-added activities for an organization to deliver value at the shortest sustainable lead time.

Kanban

Kanban is a popular Lean methodology that is widely used by several organizations. It is a

visual workflow management method for effectively managing work.

Kanban visualizes both the workflow process and work items flowing through the workflow. The visual representation of work items on a **Kanban board** allows team members to know the current state of every work item at any given time, thereby identifying potential bottlenecks in the process flow. Thus, with the Kanban approach, the development team can proactively fix the potential impediments so work items can continually flow through the states at an optimal speed. Kanban boards are visible to all stakeholders and represent a **real-time state** of work within a team or a portfolio.

In the 1940s, **Taiichi Ohno**, a Japanese industrial engineer, introduced this unique system to manage work and control inventory at every stage of production at **Toyota**. This method was part of the Toyota Production System. Later in 2004, **David J. Anderson**, a thought leader, introduced Kanban to **software development** organizations and the knowledge industry. He defined the **principles of Kanban** as below:

- Start with what you are doing now
- Agree to pursue incremental and evolutionary change

- Respect current roles and responsibilities
- Encourage acts of leadership at all levels

Start with what you are doing now

The Kanban method can be applied to any **existing** process or workflow. Kanban does not prescribe any specific set-up or roles to get started. Adopting Kanban does not need a major change to your existing process.

Agree to pursue incremental and evolutionary change

The team or the organization must align that the existing process or workflow needs an **incremental and evolutionary change**. Without a need to improve existing processes or workflows, there won't be adequate support or motivation to deploy the Kanban method.

Respect current roles and responsibilities

Kanban recognizes that there may be value in existing **processes, roles, job titles, and responsibilities** and does not prescribe any drastic changes to the existing structure. This makes the adoption of Kanban easier.

Encourage acts of leadership at all levels
This principle states that we should encourage acts of leadership at all levels within an organization, portfolio, department, or team.

"Introducing a radical change is harder than incrementally improving an existing one."
- *David J. Anderson*

The core Kanban practices that enable teams to apply Lean principles are listed as follows:

- Visualize the flow of work
- Limit WIP (Work in Progress)
- Manage Flow
- Make Process Policies Explicit
- Implement Feedback Loops
- Improve Collaboratively, Evolve Experimentally

Visualize the flow of work
The flow of work is visualized via a Kanban board that is updated regularly to represent the current state of the flow at any time.

Limit WIP (Work in Progress)
Limiting work in progress (WIP) restricts multi-tasking and allows the team to pick up tasks one after another. This practice to limit WIP

regulates the balance between the team capacity and incoming requests. It encourages the team to complete the work that they have started.

Manage Flow
The flow should be monitored at each stage to ensure smooth movement of work. Managing the flow will **establish a cadence** to monitor the average lead and cycle time, maximize value delivery, and eliminate waste.

Make Process Policies Explicit
This simply means writing up the principles and **making them visible** on the board. The great thing about making policies explicit is that people start to **respect the policies** and understand the process better.

Implement Feedback Loops
This practice focuses on **feedback loops**. Daily stand-ups in front of the Kanban board and weekly system demos enable early feedback while the 'context' is still active.

Improve Collaboratively, Evolve Experimentally
Kanban encourages an **experimental approach** where teams improve collaboratively. **Plan-Do-Check-Act (PDCA)**

is an effective model for continuous improvement via experimentation.

Exercise 1: Test your knowledge

- What is Lean? What is Kanban?
- What are the 5 Lean principles?
- What are the 7 Lean principles of Software Development?

Exercise 2: Brainstorming

Brainstorm with your team, segment data, and list down at least 3 changes that the team can make to adopt lean thinking.

*Read or listen to my other book in this series, **The Basics Of Kanban**, to learn all about the Lean Kanban framework.*

Also, read my blog "Kanban Boards – Practical Examples" for additional samples of Kanban Boards at https://authoraditiagarwal.com

Chapter 7 – House of Lean

"Start where you are. Use what you have. Do what you can."
- *Arthur Ashe*

This chapter covers the House of Lean, its purpose, and its popular versions that are being leveraged by several manufacturing and knowledge organizations.

What is the House of Lean?

The **House of Lean** is a visual representation of the Lean principles and strategies that depicts a proper way to implement Lean in any organization, portfolio, or team. Like a house is built on a strong foundation, lean concepts must also be implemented on a strong foundation. For a house to stand strong, the foundation is built first, then walls, and finally the roof. Similarly, there is a structured way to implement lean or build the house of lean.

The Toyota House of Lean

The original version of the House of Lean, also known as the **Toyota House of Lean**, is based on two pillars: **Just-in-Time** and **Jidoka**. The first pillar of the Toyota House, **Just-in-Time**, is based on manufacturing only what is needed, when it is needed, and in the quantities needed. This concept is realized by establishing a pull system to maintain a continuous flow and to eliminate waste.

The second pillar, **Jidoka**, is based on the concept that work should stop immediately when a problem first occurs. This concept was originally founded by **Sakichi Toyoda** who invented a mechanical loom that stops automatically when a cotton thread breaks. In other versions of the Toyota House, this pillar is also known as **Built-in Quality**.

The foundation of the Toyota House, **Process Stability,** is strengthened by Kaizen (continuous improvement), standardized work, and Heijunka (a production leveling technique to reduce waste).

The roof of the Toyota House or the goal is to deliver the **best quality** with the **lowest cost** and the **shortest lead time**.

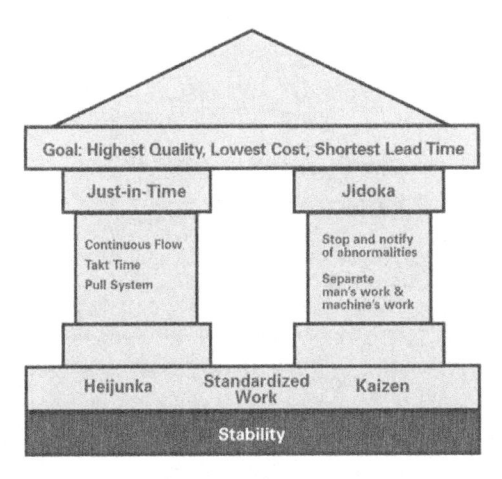

Toyota Production System "House".

(Image Source: https://www.lean.org)
Fig.1: The Toyota House of Lean

The Toyota Way 2001 House

In 2001, Toyota introduced the Toyota Way to provide a people-focused image of the house. In this image, **respect for people** and **continuous improvement** are the two strong pillars at the center. The Toyota Way 2001 represents the guiding principles at Toyota. This will continue to evolve as time progresses.

(Image Source: https://www.gray.com)
Fig.2: Toyota Way 2001 House

In Toyota Way 2001, the foundation is built on the below core values:

- Challenge
- Kaizen or continuous improvement
- Genchi Genbutsu or 'Go and See'
- Teamwork
- Respect

The first three values relate to the first pillar of continuous improvement, while the last two values relate to the second pillar of respect for people.

> *"The Toyota Production System is a practical expression of The Toyota Way – principles that guide everything we do in Toyota, based on Continuous Improvement and Respect for People."*
> - *Simon Dorrat, Toyota Manager (2008 – 2013)*

Scaled Agile Framework (SAFe) – House of Lean

As described in the book, ***SAFe 4.0 Distilled: Applying the Scaled Agile Framework for Lean Software and Systems Engineering***, the SAFe House of Lean is inspired by the Toyota House of Lean.

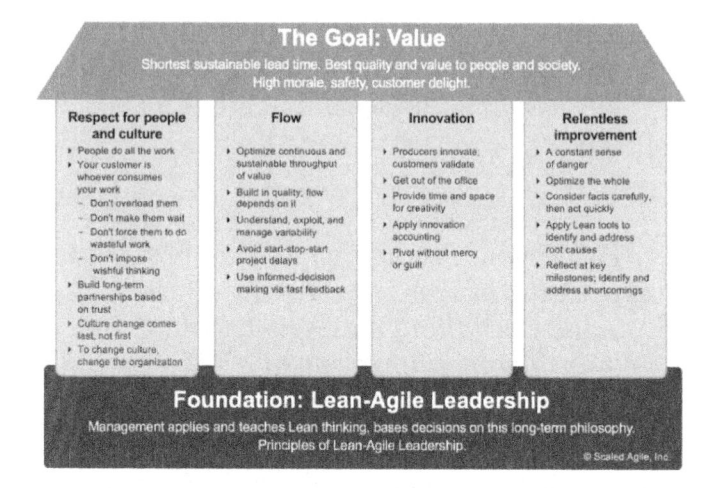

Fig.3: SAFe House of Lean
(@Scaled Agile, Inc.)

The roof of **the SAFe House of Lean** represents **value**. Lean-Agile SAFe teams strive to _deliver maximum value in the shortest sustainable lead-time._

The 4 pillars in the SAFe House of Lean are listed as follows:

- Respect for people and culture
- Flow
- Innovation
- Relentless Improvement

Respect for People and Culture:
This is one of the core values that an organization must have to be successful. Respect for each other empowers people to make decisions and learn from their mistakes. The culture of an organization should drive respect for people.

Flow
The second pillar in the SAFe House of Lean represents a continuous flow of work that is attained via limiting Work in Progress (WIP), reducing batch sizes, shorter feedback cycle, continuous integration, and continuous deployment practices. The management of continuous flow helps in reducing the blocked time and eliminating waste.

Innovation
This principle encourages people to think out-of-the-box and bring creative ideas to the table. People are encouraged to go to the actual workplace where the value is produced (Gemba) and continuously improve an existing product.

Relentless Improvement
This pillar promotes continuous learning and growth through regular retrospectives and incremental improvements. The inspect and adapt practices at key milestones highlight the

bottlenecks in the process and drive the team towards relentless improvement.

The **foundation of SAFe House of Lean** is Leadership. Without the support of an enterprise's leaders, the main goal of delivering maximum value in the shortest sustainable lead time cannot be achieved.

Note: The above section was inspired by the SAFe House of Lean (@Scaled Agile, Inc).

Exercise 1: Test your knowledge

- What is the House of Lean?//
- How many pillars are present in SAFe House of Lean?

Exercise 2: Team Discussion

- Discuss with your team if the pillars within the SAFe House of Lean are relevant to your work.
- Brainstorm with your team and list ways to embrace lean principles.

*Read or listen to my other book in this series, **<u>The Basics Of Kanban</u>**, to learn all about the Lean Kanban framework.*

If you learned something from this book, please submit your honest review on Amazon.

Chapter 8 – Agile or Lean

"Intelligence is the ability to adapt to change."
- *Stephen Hawking*

Both Agile and Lean methodologies are wildly popular these days. More and more organizations are adopting Agile and Lean practices. However, many teams struggle to describe the similarities and differences between the two. The question is: Are you Agile? Are you Lean? Can you be both?

The primary focus of Agile is to provide maximum business value via incremental and iterative development, while the primary focus of Lean is to improve existing processes, eliminate waste, and optimize the flow.

Both methodologies are different. Can they co-exist? Large Agile organizations are leveraging Lean methods to scale Agile to the enterprise. With Lean, the entire system is organized into different sequential or parallel value streams that are then optimized to improve the flow efficiency of the system as a whole. Today, Agile teams are adopting Lean thinking.

The best-suited methodology is **Lean** for:

- Improving operational efficiencies
- Performing repetitive tasks with shortest sustainable lead time
- Improving existing processes
- Eliminating waste
- Optimizing the end-to-end flow
- Maximizing productivity
- Reducing the average lead time
- Reduce the average cycle time

The best-suited methodology is **Agile** for:

- Promoting frequent customer collaboration
- Supporting emergent design
- Adapting to change

- Delivering the highest business value
- Developing incrementally
- Driving innovation

Both Lean and Agile will work for:

- Driving Quality
- Creating a culture of collaboration, trust, and respect for each other
- Just-in-Time development
- Continuous Improvement
- Making decisions at the Last Responsible Moment (LRM)

Similarities in Agile and Lean

Some of the core similarities between Agile and Lean are listed as follows:

Development approach
Lean development encourages reducing the batch size and limit work-in-progress (WIP). Agile methodology, too, promotes prioritization of work items and incremental development of working software within short, time-boxed iterations.

Continuous Improvement
Lean development is very focused on **Kaizen** or continuous improvement. Agile development

also signifies the importance of the **inspect and adapt** activities such as product demo and retrospectives that promote continuous improvement.

Collaboration

Teamwork is one of the core values defined in Toyota Way 2001. The Lean methodology encourages collaboration between team members. Agile development, too, has a strong focus on people interactions and collaboration with product stakeholders. The below two values stated in the Agile Manifesto reflect the same.

- Individuals and interactions over processes and tools
- Customer collaboration over contract negotiation

Moreover, the 4th Agile principle, *'Business people and developers must work together daily throughout the project.'* is also focused on collaboration.

Customer-centric approach

Lean is a customer-centric methodology that focuses to deliver the best quality and value in the shortest sustainable lead-time. Agile methodology is also centered on the customer. The 1st Agile principle, *'Our highest priority is to satisfy the customer through early and continuous delivery of valuable software.'*, is written with a customer-first approach.

Just-in-Time approach
Both Agile and Lean methodologies encourage the Just-in-Time approach. One of the two pillars in the Toyota House of Lean is '**Just-in-Time**' that encourages to produce only what is needed, when it is needed, and in the quantities needed. Agile development, too, promotes 'Just-in-Time' planning, design, development, and documentation. Agile encourages teams to refine, design, and document only the prioritized work items. Agile concepts such as incremental development and emergent design reinforce the 'Just-in-Time' approach.

Waste Elimination
Though Lean is the major proponent for waste elimination, Agile methodology, too, supports this concept by delaying decisions until **the last responsible moment (LRM)**. Thus, with LRM, possible rework, caused when working on an incorrect feature or an incorrect design, is minimized.

Differences in Agile and Lean

Let's look at some of the core differences between Agile and Lean.

Origin
Lean management was originated in the manufacturing sector to reduce waste and improve the efficiency of the existing system, whereas Agile methodology was conceived by the software development thinkers to solve problems with the traditional software development approach.

Nature of work
Lean methodology is best suited to optimize simple, repetitive tasks that flow through different workflow states. On the contrary, Agile is best suited to build complex products that require research, experimentation, the ability to adapt to change, and collaboration.

End Goal
With Lean, the end goal is to deliver a high-quality product in the shortest sustainable lead-time, in the most economical way, while eliminating redundancies and waste. With Agile, the end goal is to deliver the maximum business value, respond quickly to the changing business needs, and develop incrementally in an iterative way.

Team Size
Lean methodology is applied to improve processes in large enterprises and teams. **Value stream mapping** helps to visualize the end-

to-end journey or steps required to deliver value to the customer. On the other hand, Agile is most effective when applied to small teams with a team size of 5-8 people.

Exercise 1: Test your knowledge

- What are the core similarities between Agile and Lean methodologies?

- What are the main differences between Agile and Lean methodologies?

Exercise 2: Team Discussion

Which methodology will be best suited for your organization or team?

Learn all about Agile Scrum with my other bestselling book, ***The Basics Of Scrum – A Simple Handbook to the Most Popular Agile Scrum Framework.***

Bibliography

LeSS Framework. "Lean Thinking". LeSS.
https://less.works/less/principles/lean-thinking.html

Agile Alliance. "Agile 101". Agile Alliance. 2019.
https://www.agilealliance.org/agile101/

Scaled Agile. "SAFe for Lean Enterprises"
Scaled Agile Inc. 2019.
https://www.scaledagileframework.com/

Scott Ambler. "The Disciplined Agile Manifesto". Disciplined Agile Consortium.
https://www.disciplinedagiledelivery.com

Michael Balle. TPS or the Toyota Way?
Lean.org. 2015.
https://www.lean.org/LeanPost/Posting.cfm?LeanPostId=514

Recommended Reading

- *Lean Software Development by Mary Poppendieck and Tom Poppendieck*

- *SAFe 4.5 Distilled: Applying the Scaled Agile Framework for Lean Enterprises by Richard Knaster and Dean Leffingwell*

- *Kanban: Successful Evolutionary Change for Your Technology Business by David Anderson*

- *Essential Scrum: A Practical Guide to the Most Popular Agile Process by Kenneth S. Rubin*

- *Scrum: The Art of Doing Twice the Work in Half the Time by Jeff Sutherland and JJ Sutherland*

- *Agile Estimating and Planning by Mike Cohn*

- *The Lean Startup: How Today's Entrepreneurs Use Continuous Innovation to Create Radically Successful Businesses* by Eric Ries

- *Lean Thinking: Banish Waste and Create Wealth in Your Corporation* by James P. Womack and Daniel T. Jones

- *User Stories Applied: For Agile Software Development* by Mike Cohn

- *Strategize: Product Strategy and Product Roadmap Practices for the Digital Age* by Roman Pichler

- *Leading Change* by John P. Kotter

- *The Lean Machine: How Harley-Davidson Drove Top-Line Growth and Profitability with Revolutionary Lean Product Development* by Dantar P. Oosterwal

- *The Rollout: A Novel about Leadership and Building a Lean-Agile Enterprise with SAFe®* by Alex Yakyma

About Me

Aditi Agarwal is an experienced Agile Coach, a certified SAFe Process Consultant, a certified Scrum Master, and a published author. She is very excited to share her knowledge with her readers. Her mission is to spread knowledge, positivity, love, and compassion in the world.

Aditi lives in Phoenix, AZ with her loving family. She likes to travel, read, write, and meet new people. Aditi writes short books in a straight-forward and easy-to-understand language such that readers can derive maximum value without investing a lot of their time into reading bulky books.

More Books by the Author

1. *The Basics Of SCRUM: A Simple Handbook to the Most Popular Agile Scrum Framework*

   *This book explains the **Scrum** roles, artifacts, ceremonies, and principles, along with advanced concepts such as managing technical debt, writing good user stories, publishing scrum charts, and more. The Basics Of Scrum will be useful to those who want to learn Scrum and expand their career opportunities, or those who don't have time to read bulky books and thus need a simple reference book on Scrum.*

2. *The Basics Of Kanban: A Popular Lean Framework*

   *This book is written to provide you with a complete reference guide on **Kanban**. Learn how to effectively manage your* *personal and professional work with the Lean Kanban framework.*

3. <u>Enterprise Agility with OKRs: A Complete Guide to Enterprise Business Agility</u>

   Enterprises must achieve "true agility" to sustain businesses and drive outcomes in this fast-paced, competitive, and rapidly changing environment.

   This book is specially designed for thought leaders who are leading agile transformation efforts, coaching agile or lean frameworks, implementing **OKRs**, *or bringing more* **business agility** *to their enterprise.*

4. <u>An Expert Guide to Problem Solving – With Practical Examples</u>

   This book will give you an understanding of the different problem-solving tools such as **Fishbone Diagram, Brainstorming, Failure Modes and Effects Analysis, SWOT matrix, and 5Whys** *along* *with practical examples and applications of these tools.*

5. <u>Emerging Technology Trends: Frequently Asked Questions</u>

   *This book covers frequently asked questions about emerging technology trends such as **Blockchain, Bitcoin, Ethereum, Ripple, Artificial Intelligence, Machine Learning, Artificial Neural Networks, Deep Learning, Augmented Reality, Connected Homes, Quantum Computing,** and more.*

6. <u>Harness The Power Within: Unleash your Inner Strength with Faith, Patience, and a Positive Mind</u>

   *The purpose of this book is to **inspire** you to live a **happy** and **fulfilled life**. There's a famous quote, "We are never defeated unless we give up on God."*

7. *Embrace Positivity: Think, Speak, And Act - A 3-Step Strategy to Live Your Best Life*

   *This motivational **self-help** book reveals a 3-step strategy to embrace **positivity** in life. It emphasizes the role of positive thinking, affirmations or the spoken word, and positive actions in attaining self-esteem and success. This book can be used as a handbook or a reference book to achieve success through a positive mental attitude.*

8. *Agile Product Management Templates: Discover (+FREE Download) Agile Templates - Product Persona, Product Vision, Product Roadmap, Dependency Matrix, and the Feature Writing Checklist*
   This short book introduces my carefully crafted agile product management templates for creating product personas, product vision, and a product roadmap. This book also covers dependency matrix templates along with a checklist to write good features.

Post Your Review

*If you learned something new, please submit your **honest review** on Amazon. Your review will help me to improve the content of this book and reach a wider audience.*

***Special Thanks** for your encouragement and continued support.*

*Check out my **website** for agile and lean blog posts:
https://authoraditiagarwal.com*

Printed in Great Britain
by Amazon